ADVANCE PRAISE FOR THE BROKE BABE'S BOOK OF MAGIC

From one broke witch to another, this book is an excellent source of material to grow deeper in your practice while maintaining inclusivity and affordability. Pamalah does a brilliant job of guiding the reader through several spells/rituals while keeping it relatable and accessible.

—Katie Fruits, Animistic Green Witch, Owner and operator of Lore & Bramble

Perfect for beginners! When you're just starting out, it's hard to know what you can or can't do as a new practitioner. This book basically tells you to master the basics first before reaching higher, and it does so with your budget in mind. Highly recommend for anyone starting their journey.

—AJ Borders, Spiritual Practitioner @thebookishcousin on Insta&Tiktok

The Broke Babe's
Book of Magic

An Inclusive Beginner's Guide to Affordable Witchcraft

Pamalah Johnson

Printed and bound in the United States of America

ISBN: 979-8-218-81855-5

DEDICATION

Big thanks and love to …

My fabulous parents, Kamalah and Doug Gordon

My wonderfully amazing Aquarius Brother

My hurricane Capricorn Sister

My hilarious Taurus and Leo Nephews

My Capricorn best friend of 26 years, Megan

ABOUT THE AUTHOR

I am a Bay Area–born root worker, deeply rooted in the traditions of Hoodoo and the Voodoo religion—with an American soul and ancestral fire guiding my path. Through tarot, cartomancy, and spell work, I walk the crossroads between spirit and self, offering insight, healing, and empowerment to those who seek.

I am here to build a community that uplifts and protects—one that honors the spirits, respects the roots, and welcomes all who align with justice, freedom, and love.

I am unapologetically: Pro-Black. Pro-Minority. Pro-LGBTQIA+. Pro-Women. Pro-Choice. Pro-Palestinian. I stand with the marginalized. I believe in liberation.

If your heart beats for justice, you belong here.

With love, solidarity, and sacred resistance.

"If you are always trying to be normal,
you will never know how amazing you can be"
- Maya Angelou

CONTENTS

FOREWORD BY LINDSEY MELNICK

I first met Pamalah through giving her a reading, and even then it was so clear that she carried something special. I remember encouraging her to dive deeper into her gifts and to share them with the world, because her presence was too healing, too full of joy, to be kept quiet. To see her now, stepping forward with this book, feels like a beautiful continuation of that calling and she has embraced it with courage and grace.

In every interaction, she embodies the kind of presence that makes people feel safe, seen, and uplifted. She approaches her craft not only with wisdom, but with a rare warmth and generosity of spirit. This book reflects that same energy as a guide, a companion, and a gentle reminder that spirituality is not something far away, but something we can live and breathe each day.

As you read her words, I trust you'll feel her joy and her healing touch woven into every page. May this book meet you exactly where you are, and open a doorway into the deeper connection, clarity, and magic that she so effortlessly inspires in others.

Pamalah, I am so beyond proud of you. Thank you for sharing your healing with us.

—Lindsay Melnick, "The Florida Witch",
Clairvoyant Psychic and Tarot reader

INTRODUCTION

Dear witchy, spiritual, or curious reader,
This quick and simple spell, recipe, and guide-book embodies two of my core values: spirituality is not a luxury—it should be accessible to all, regardless of income. Magical discoveries and callings can happen at any age whether you're 13 or 105. A beginner witch can bloom at any stage of life. This book offers magical spells, practices, and cleanses with cost in mind. It's meant to be an uncomplicated, quick reference. You can always add more ingredients if you wish, but remember, dear reader: the ingredients and tools are not what make the magic—you do. The power is within you; everything else is just an aid.

Now go forth and make your world more magical.

Though I am a root worker (Hoodoo) and practice American Voodoo, this book does not include those specific practices. These are closed traditions that I do not share publicly at this time. I am still in conversation with my ancestors and spirits, seeking guidance on how and when to share that part of my path.

Go forth and make your
world more magical.

1: Your Chosen Practice

WHAT TYPE OF WITCH?

You might be wondering, "What type of witch am I meant to be? And is it important to know?"

I'll preface by saying a lot of witches have their hands in many different forms of spiritual practices—and that's completely natural. As your craft grows, your knowledge of each one will grow too.

However, you'll likely feel a natural pull toward certain aspects of the craft. These may be things you've always been drawn to without realizing it, or things you've recently discovered that deeply resonate with you.

I don't believe in taking those online quizzes to "find out what kind of witch you are." I think that's completely unnecessary. Instead, educate yourself on the different types of witches and see if anything calls to you naturally.

Depending on your cultural background, it may be hard to pinpoint exactly what kind of witch you are, because your heritage will also influence your practice.

Some may classify me as a hedge or kitchen witch, but I would say that's more a reflection of my strong Hoodoo and Voodoo roots. I'm a natural-born divination witch and showed signs of it early in childhood. That kind of calling shows up in different ways, depending on the person.

What I'm really saying is follow that natural pull. It's often indescribable, but it's how you know what you're being called to. And that's the path you need to learn more about.

Follow that natural pull. It's often indescribable, but it's how you know what you're being called to.

COVEN OR NO COVEN?

I think this depends on how much of a traditionalist you are and your personality type. In general, witchcraft can be a very solitary practice, with gatherings with the coven reserved for special occasions.

More social witches who prefer practicing in a group setting may even meet weekly or monthly. I personally practice witchcraft almost entirely alone, but I'm also the leader of a small coven I created that gathers a few times a year.

I do think it's important to build a sisterhood, gathering to provide counsel, share spells and ingredients, and perform spells and rituals to better the coven and the world. I'm all for coming together for a good group hex to make it more powerful.

And yes, you can have a closed practice and still be part of a coven. (See "What is a Closed Practice?" in chapter 13.) As you can see throughout this book, I was able to share spells without including any type of Hoodoo or Voodoo ingredients.

———••••⊗••••———

It's important to build a sisterhood.
Gathering to provide counsel, share spells
and ingredients, and perform spells and
rituals to better the coven and the world.

———••••⊗••••———

CASUAL WITCHCRAFT?

Another question that might arise is this: "Can I casually practice witchcraft?"

Like religion, your practice may ebb and flow. Some people practice daily, others only during major events or at specific times. I'm not here to judge your journey or how you choose to practice. You shouldn't let anyone else, either. My note is to at least keep up with small spiritual practices like cleansing your home. Spirits, ancestors, or the gods may find some disrespect if you call upon them only when you need something, so just keep that in mind.

———••••⊗••••———

Your practice may ebb and flow.

———••••⊗••••———

2: Supplies

When I started to lean more into my craft and roots, I was overwhelmed with what to get and what to buy. I'm the type who buys it all just to make sure I'm not missing a single thing—which, to be honest, cost me a pretty penny. I don't want other witches leaning into their craft to drop a dime like I did. So, I've curated a list of things I use often that have helped strengthen my craft and spells.

YOUR POT

I have a separate pot specifically for witchcraft. Why, you may ask? Cross-contamination with food items. Safety still needs to be followed—even in witchcraft.

Cooking food in the same pot you do spell work is dangerous. For a low-cost option, I suggest getting a secondhand pot or using a well-worn one you no longer cook with.

If you do get a pot secondhand, I suggest cleansing it. Here are a few quick ways:

Option 1: Boil water (Moon water* if you have it), bring it to a simmer, and add lemon and Florida Water.* Then strain, rinse, and dry.

*Information on Moon water and Florida Water can be found in chapter 7 of this book.

Option 2: Light an incense stick, swirl it clockwise three times around the pot, then wipe the inside and outside with Florida Water. Rinse and dry.

Option 3: Rinse, wash, and dry the pot with Moon water.

As you cleanse the pot, say aloud:

"I call for cleansing of this object."

Repeat this three to six times.

Bonus: You can light a white candle during the cleansing.

HEAT-SAFE BOWLS, PLATES, AND CUPS

As I mentioned above, I strongly recommend using items for witchcraft separate from anything you would typically eat or drink from. These can be items you already have, secondhand finds, or inexpensive new ones. The key is that they should be heat-resistant.

Often in spell work, you'll write on a piece of paper or a bay leaf and burn it. You'll need something safe to place it on or in. I've found ashtrays to be an affordable and heat-tolerant option. Remember, you're usually burning small things—strips/folded paper or bay leaves—so big flames shouldn't occur.

Some practitioners like to use cups or plates instead. No matter what your choice, always use fire with caution and follow safe practices.

Disclaimer: Just because I use an ashtray doesn't mean I'm advising you to do the same. Please do your own research and proceed at your own risk. I always keep water, salt, or a fire extinguisher nearby—just in case.

MASON JARS AND SPRAY BOTTLES

I find jars essential to witchcraft. I collect glass jars of all shapes and sizes. Mason jars tend to be the most versatile. Buying them in bulk can be pricey, but they'll last a long time. You can also find jars at thrift stores, goodwill, and garage sales.

Why jars?

They're fantastic for storing herbs, Moon water, cleansing brews, and spell jars. Plus, they come with excellent sealing lids.

Some practitioners also like to use small glass apothecary bottles for their anointing and carrier oils. These usually come with droppers, which are ideal—but they can get expensive. I suggest doing more research if making or storing oils is something you're really interested in. Otherwise, you might end up buying supplies you don't need or won't use often.

If you're drawn to working with oils, take the time to explore that path more deeply.

SPRAY BOTTLES

Are spray bottles absolutely essential? No. But they do make things a lot easier—especially when it comes to spraying Florida Water or homemade brews.

For example, I store rose water in a spray bottle to spritz around my home. I also keep small spray bottles of Florida Water for cleansing myself, my tools, and my space before readings. It's something I love because I can take it with me on the go.

I suggest buying one large spray bottle and two to three small ones. They're generally very affordable.

PLASTIC VS. GLASS

I often get asked whether it's okay to use plastic jars and spray bottles. My answer? Absolutely. I'm not here to judge or be an elitist. Do whatever is most cost-effective for you.

If you want a more polished look or something that stores well long-term, go for glass. But if plastic is what you can afford—or if you're not sure how deep you'll go into making sprays—plastic is completely fine.

Note: If you plan to dip your jar in warm (not hot) wax to seal a jar spell, I 100-percent recommend using glass. In my experience, plastic doesn't support the process as well.

CANDLE HOLDERS

Candle holders will be a must if you plan on using tapers for your magic practice. Traditional tapers used in magic are about 5 to 6 inches long. You *can* use longer tapers, which take more time to burn, but the upside is you can use them more than once. With that being said, you'll have to decide what kind of taper holder you'd like. I collect all shapes and sizes because I love to burn them for magic as well as decorate my home with them.

Some people prefer to use pillar candles, which only need to be placed on a heat-safe plate, or they'll buy prayer candles in different colors based on the spell. I'm a huge candle lover, so I use almost all forms of candles. Candle holders are traditionally pretty inexpensive, and you can often thrift them.

I personally invested in taper holders that also have a protective glass around them to shield the flame from outside elements that aren't magic-based, like the wind—and of course, for overall candle safety. I come from a retail background selling candles, so I'm all about fire safety.

I don't suggest buying the type of taper candle holder I use unless this is something you're truly invested in.

INCENSE BURNER

Much like candles, incense is very popular in the spiritual and magical world. They assist with spells and help create a certain type of environment. For example, burning lavender incense to help protect your space. Incense holders are extremely inexpensive. You'll come across small ones made for cone-shaped incense or long stick incense. Both are affordable—I use both styles.

Note: Like candles, I know some individuals—and even pets—can be sensitive to incense. The good news is, there are other ways to create a fragrance and set the mood without having to burn anything. Fragrance can help amplify the energy of a spell, but it's not required.

For a gentler option, humidifiers that mist essential oils can be a great alternative. You can also use a simple mist spray made with essential oils. And of course, you don't have to use fragrance at all. It's always optional—but it can enhance the magic in your space.

ALTAR CLOTH

I suggest using altar cloths, and you can even make your own or customize one using arts and craft supplies. The cloth serves as a dedicated, protective area for your spell work. It usually goes on top of your altar, but it can also travel with you. Many come with protective symbols already printed on them, or you can draw or add more. I always recommend spraying your cloth with a Florida Water mist or other cleansing spray before starting spell work.

Now of course, I don't speak in absolutes—you don't have to use an altar cloth every time. Personally, in my own practice, I don't always use one. For example, if the objects I'm using for the spell already have protective symbols and have been properly cleansed, I don't mind working directly on that surface. I also surround my altar objects with salt and cleansing herbs regardless.

Also, magic can be done anytime, anywhere, so you may not always have an altar cloth with you. If that's the case, I suggest creating a protective circle using herbs, flowers, spices (if you have them), and of course, salt.

ALTAR PLATE

I'm a big fan of using an altar plate. Once again, you can make anything into an altar plate—just make sure it's heat-safe, or you can purchase one. I place my candles on top of the plate and surround them with trinkets, charms, or whatever else I want to include in that spell. I also use it to place my offerings.

Now, my altar is large, so I also place things directly on the altar cloth. But for things I want to emphasize, I place them on the altar plate. Like anything else, before setting up for a spell or offering, I make sure to wash and cleanse the plate to reset it. You may not find something labeled specifically as an altar plate, but thrifted dishes or plates work just as well.

Note: See also chapter 14 for input on outdoor altar setups.

YOUR BELLS

Bells are traditionally used in two ways within the spiritual world when it comes to witchcraft and spiritual practice.

1. As a way to protect the home and ward off evil or those with bad intentions. They can also serve as a warning.
2. During a spell or when honoring spirits, gods, and ancestors, you may ring a bell to call them in.

I don't personally believe ringing bells is a must, but it is something I do every time. I know my spirits, ancestors, and gods are always with me, but that doesn't mean they're constantly working with me or helping me out. Ringing the bell is kind of a way to say, "Hey, I need your attention," even if it's just to honor and thank them at my altar.

Make sure to call them in a respectful and caring way. They are here to assist and guide you, but you must never take advantage of them or their time. Just like us, they enjoy eating, drinking, and being merry.

I personally crafted individual bells for my door and outside of my home—I'm into art and crafting, so I take any chance I get to create something. You can also buy these pre-made ones at a spiritual shop. I also bought a bell separately. As mentioned before, Etsy is a great resource for witchcraft supplies and you're supporting small businesses when you shop there.

Note: As your practice grows, you'll decide for yourself which supplies you need and which ones you don't. The list above includes items I've personally found myself using in almost every single spell—or just in my everyday witch life. See also chapter 14 for more input on where to shop for supplies.

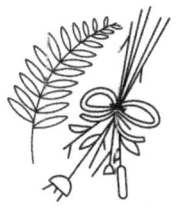

3: Herbs, Flowers, Spices, and More

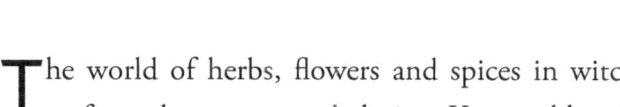

The world of herbs, flowers and spices in witch-craft can be very overwhelming. You could easily spend years learning the ins and outs of how each one is used within the craft.

When I first started, I wasn't sure which herbs I actually *needed*—so I bought them in bulk.

Do I regret that decision? Not necessarily.

Are there herbs and flowers I'll probably never use? Yes.

That's why I came up with this quick guide:

A list of herbs, flowers, and spices (and a few other things) that I personally use often. Many of these are lower in cost, easy to find, and can be bought in bulk and stored for a long time.

I've also included a short description of what each herb, flower, and spice is commonly used for, to help you build your own collection more intentionally.

COLOR-CODED SYSTEM FOR SPELLS

Since I want this to be a quick reference guide, I'm going to list this in a color-coded system—a method I use for my own research when I need a quick reference. Next to each herb, flower, space, and other items, I'll write a color that coordinates with the subject it helps with. This way, when you need to quickly reference what the use is for, you just have to look at the color.

Black – Hex

Blue – Divination, spirit connection, and amplified clairvoyance

Green – Luck, fortune, and wealth

Pink – Love (which references all forms of love—self-love, romantic love, platonic love, and creating love in your environment)

Yellow – Protection, cleansing, and balance

Just a reminder, these are quick outlines of what these do. You can always dive deeper into each one if you'd like; these are just a quick reference. And remember, the magic is within you, so if you don't have any of these ingredients on hand, don't worry. These just amplify the spell. The result comes from the energy and intuition that you're putting into it.

HERBS

Bay leaves/Bay Laurel – *Blue and Yellow*

Dill – *Blue and Pink*

Catnip – *Blue, Green and Pink* (I use it for cat magic)

Oregano – *Blue and Green*

Rosemary – *Blue and Yellow*

FLOWERS

Lavender – *Blue and Yellow*

Jasmine – *Blue and Pink*

Roses (petals or whole) – *Blue, Green and Pink*

Chamomile – *Green, Pink, and Yellow*

WILDFLOWERS AND RANDOM OUTSIDE FLOWERS

Sometimes I just pick fresh random flowers and bring them to my altar. I use them to represent the energy of the outside and nature. Using fresh energy to help amplify, cleanse, and reboot the altar's energy.

SPICES

Allspice – *Green*
Cinnamon – *Pink and Yellow*
Clove – *Blue, Pink and Yellow*
Nutmeg – *Green*

FRUIT

Lemon – *Yellow*
Orange – *Blue, Green, and Yellow*

MIXED FRUITS

These are offerings and thank-yous to my ancestors, spirits, and god/goddesses.

MISCELLANEOUS

Salt – *Yellow*

Spicy food powder (Chilli, Cayenne, etc.) – ***Black and Yellow***

Note: I have excluded certain items from this list because I use them in my closed practice.

This quick guide is a combination of my own knowledge and information I found in the book *Herbal Magic* by Aurora Kane. It's a great resource with a helpful breakdown of different herbs and their uses—I often reference it during my spell research as a cross-reference. That said, I'd only recommend getting this book if you truly want to dive deeper into herbal magic and knowledge. Some of the herbs listed (and many more in the book) aren't ones you'll necessarily use in everyday magic. I don't want you buying unnecessary supplies unless you're sure you want to do a specific spell or have a clear use in mind.

Go to www.ladybugdivinationandspells.com to download a free, colorful reference sheet you can print out and keep with your herbs and candles to refer to as you work.

4: Candle Guide

Candles are an absolute staple in witchcraft, Hoodoo, and Voodoo.

They can be used in nearly every type of spell, and there are even witches who specialize purely in candle magic.

Personally, I light a candle for almost every magical working I do. Even during glamour magic—which is highlighted later in this book—I light a candle while preparing the ingredients. In general, I have a candle burning almost every day, whether it's a regular candle for ambience and scent, or one used for witchcraft, rootwork, or my spiritual practices in American Voodoo.

WHY CANDLE COLORS MATTER

In spiritual practice and witchcraft, candle colors traditionally represent intent, the type of spell being performed, or the deity (god/goddess) you're working with.

Below, I've highlighted the most common candle colors and their traditional meanings.

Most spell candles tend to be shorter taper candles, but let me be clear—there are no absolutes in this craft. I personally use:

- Tealights
- Votive candles
- Floating candles

Use what works best for you and your practice.

FLAME-FREE ALTERNATIVES

I also want to acknowledge that not everyone can use open flames. If you or someone you live with are sensitive to smoke, or you have pets, or you just can't have fire in your space, don't worry.

Battery-operated flickering candles are a great alternative.

They even come in different colors.

And let me be perfectly clear:

You are not any less of a witch for using flame-free candles.

Because why?

The magic is in YOU.

I will keep repeating that.

A NOTE ON WHITE CANDLES

If you don't have access to a wide range of candle colors that's okay.

The most traditional and versatile candle color is white.

White can be used for any kind of spell or magical working. When I don't have the color I need, I simply carve my intention into the candle. I often use a small, inexpensive clay sculpting tool (meant for pottery) to carve words, phrases, or symbols directly into the wax.

———•••• ◈ ••••———

The magic is in YOU.

———•••• ◈ ••••———

DRESSING AND ANOINTING CANDLES

There are amazing books and online resources that go into dressing and anointing candles, how to prepare them with oils, herbs, or powders depending on your intention.

Because I mix both Voodoo and Hoodoo ingredients when dressing my candles and because some of that is sacred and specific to my path—I won't be listing those here. But rest assured, if you want to explore that further, there are plenty of resources out there for diving deeper into the art of candle preparation.

I *will*, however, share the steps I take to dress or anoint candles with oil.

I mix all my ingredients together in a bowl or on a plate. Then I take a few drops of oil and rub it all over the taper candle. After that, I sprinkle the mixed ingredients over the candle. I don't drown my candle in oil as this can become a safety issue when it's lit. Once it's dressed, I place the candle in the candle holder.

This method can also be used for tea lights, votives, or floating candles. I personally don't add oil or extra herbs or mix to candles that are enclosed in glass. I practice witchcraft, but I also prioritize safety in my environment.

Note: I love using wax adapters, or wax "ointment" that goes at the bottom of the candle to keep it in place inside the holder.

CANDLE COLOR GUIDE FOR WITCHCRAFT

Candles are powerful magical tools used across countless traditions. Color can amplify your intention—but remember, white candles can stand in for *any* color if that's what you have. Your intention matters more than the tools.

Use this guide to choose your candle color—or carve into a plain candle to set your purpose.

COMMON CANDLE COLORS AND THEIR MEANINGS

Color	Intentions/Uses
White	All-purpose. Purity, cleansing, protection, spiritual work, peace, ancestors.
Black	Banishing, hexing, uncrossing, protection, absorbing negativity, ancestral work.
Red	Passion, power, strength, courage, lust, fast action, motivation, sexual energy.

Pink   Self-love, romance, emotional healing, friendship, soft energy, beauty work.

Blue   Calm, clarity, truth, emotional healing, dreams, communication.

Green   Prosperity, luck, money, success, fertility, nature magic, abundance.

Yellow   Confidence, focus, creativity, intellect, joy, attraction, solar energy.

Orange   Road opening,* fast success, energy boosts, changing circumstances.

Purple   Wisdom, psychic ability, spiritual power, divination, commanding energy.

Brown   Grounding, stability, home, pets, earthly connections.

Gold   Solar deities, wealth, divine masculine, ambition, victory.

Silver   Lunar work, intuition, divine feminine, Moon magic, reflection.

*Note: For more on road-opening candles, see chapter 10.

Go to www.ladybugdivinationandspells.com to download a free, colorful reference sheet you can print out and keep with your herbs and candles to refer to as you work.

Note: In this chapter, I chose not to include a recommended book for further reading and education. That is because candle magic is incredibly vast and full of information. You could easily find yourself spending money on multiple books, only to end up feeling overwhelmed and confused.

Personally, I suggest starting with some light online research. See what resonates with you and then decide if it's something you want to explore more deeply. This approach lets you ease in and save some money up front.

(Please also see chapter 14 for input on candle issues that might arise.)

5: Tarot: A Simple Introduction

Tarot, much like astrology, can be very detailed and overwhelming. In this section, I'm going to provide a very watered-down, simple way to get started mixed with my personal journey and what I did.

I started off with one tarot deck and let me tell you: the energy between you and your tarot deck is so important. This is a connection to your magic, your spirits, your ancestors, and even your god or gods. I find it to be a deeply spiritual connection to my roots, my personal magic, and my divination practice.

I strongly believe there is a synergistic relationship that builds between you and your cards over time. Their energy becomes yours, and your energy becomes theirs. In spirituality and witchcraft, it's all about the energy around you and within you.

In my personal tarot journey, I followed a consistent system to help me get used to the practice. Over time, I built a rapport with my cards, and now I feel comfortable being more intuitive with my process rather than sticking to the same exact routine each time.

⸻⸰◈◦⸻

In spirituality and witchcraft, it's all about the energy around you and within you.

⸻⸰◈◦⸻

GETTING STARTED

If this is a brand-new deck, I recommend immediately taking the cards and, with the deck face down, flipping some of them in different directions (upright and reversed). Then begin the shuffling process, described below:

STEPS:

- Shuffle the deck several times until it feels right. This feeling is hard to describe—it's an energetic signal you'll come to recognize over time.

- Knock on the deck three times, then shuffle one more time. Separate the deck into three piles. Pick up the piles in no particular order.
- Spread the cards out face down and pick the ones that are calling to you. I typically do a three-card spread and flip them to my left.
- This spread usually represents Past, Present, and Future—one of the most common and beginner-friendly layouts.

When I started, I didn't know what any of the cards meant. That's why I made sure to choose a deck that included clear explanations, either printed directly on the cards or in the guidebook. Over the years, I've experimented with different ways to lay the cards out.

If you're interested in exploring more advanced spreads or reading styles after getting comfortable with your first deck, I recommend purchasing a more detailed tarot book. But before investing in anything, check in with yourself:

Do you actually enjoy tarot?

As with everything in this guide, the goal is to reduce costs on your spiritual journey. So hold off on buying extra materials until you know tarot is something you truly want to dive deeper into.

ADDITIONAL TAROT INFORMATION

You can be direct when asking your tarot deck questions. Here are some thoughtful examples:

- Is there anything I need to know at this moment?
- What would you say my current emotional state is?
- Can you provide me with some life advice?
- I'm stuck in my career—what should I do?

You'd be surprised by the insights the cards can offer. Sometimes the answer is very direct; other times, it might ask you to sit with your emotions and reflect.

Some practitioners find it helpful to keep a dedicated tarot journal—writing down which cards appear and how they feel about them. I highly recommend this if you're looking to deepen your connection with the cards and yourself.

DOING READINGS FOR OTHERS

You don't have to read for other people—you can absolutely keep it between me, myself, and I. That said, many tarot readers do feel called to help those in need.

One question I often get is: Do you use your personal deck to read for others?

I've had a bit of a journey with this. I believe in the synergistic relationship between you and your tarot deck—it grows and deepens over time. When I first started, I used my personal deck for myself and a small circle of close people. But as that relationship evolved, it became something sacred. I no longer felt comfortable using that deck for others. So, I began using separate decks for family, friends, and clients.

The same thing is happening now with my current cartomancy deck. Now, I use it for both myself and others. But once that connection becomes personal and sacred, I'll retire it from public use and get additional decks just for reading for others.

I do want to say: the decks I use for others still carry powerful energy. I have a connection to them, too, they're just not my soul deck, as I like to call it.

I highly recommend spending time getting familiar with your cards before reading for someone else. I practiced for several days on myself before offering readings to family and close friends. Walking through the process solo helped me build confidence and deepen my connection to the cards.

And here's something important to remember:

You may also discover that tarot simply isn't for you—and that's perfectly okay.

There are many tools for divination, and part of the journey is discovering which ones speak most clearly to your spirits, ancestors, and gods/god.

CLEANSING AND CARE

I cleanse my deck regularly and keep cleansing herbs stored in the box or bag where I keep my cards. I'll also lightly spray my cards with Florida Water or a cleansing mist.

You can also light a cleansing incense and wave it gently around the deck if that feels right.

If I've done a particularly intense or emotional reading, I'll use both spray and incense—it helps reset the energy completely.

Note: If you're interested in receiving a professional reading, I invite you to visit my site at www.Ladybugdivinationandspells.com. There, you can book a session and experience a personalized reading provided by yours truly.

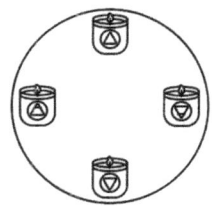

6: Calling Corners and Protective Circles

Before I get into the details of calling corners and casting protective circles, I want to preface by saying: some other practitioners might not like the way I do it and that's okay.

You'll find that there are very traditional witches who practice in a systematic, structured way. That's not a bad thing at all. Tradition has its place and provides a strong foundation.

But that's just not my style.

My craft is deeply intuitive and personal. I have respect for the roots of ritual, but I shape most of my practice around what feels aligned with me.

I'm mostly a solitary witch, with a very small coven. I perform the majority of my spells at home or on the land I live on. My space is already intentionally designed with protection and elemental balance in mind, so I don't follow a strict or formal method of calling corners each time. But let me be clear, I'm not cocky about it.

I still believe calling corners is a form of respect and a way of honoring the spirits, ancestors, gods, and guides you're calling in. So even though I don't always walk the full circle or speak long invocations, I acknowledge each direction and give thanks in my own words. I may light candles or place objects that represent each element, but I let my intuition guide how and when I do it.

PROTECTIVE CIRCLES: MY APPROACH

When it comes to casting a protective circle, I don't always cast one around myself—I typically cast it around my altar or spell setup.

Now, other practitioners might disagree with this approach, and that's okay. I personally wear protective jewelry and anoint myself with oils or sprays before spell work, so I carry that layer of protection on me at all times.

Calling corners is a form of respect and a way of honoring the spirits, ancestors, gods, and guides you're calling in.

WHAT IS "CALLING CORNERS"?

Calling corners is a way to call upon the elements, the gods, spirits, and ancestors that inhabit the North, South, East, and West. It also allows you to make the space sacred and, some would say, enter a magical state within that space.

Like casting circles, certain practitioners have exact wording they use every time, along with specific body movements. As for me—I do it a little differently, but I still call the corners most of the time when I'm doing spells.

I'm human, and honestly, sometimes I get so caught up in preparing everything else that I forget and just get started. But even then, I'm still calling on my spirits in my own way: I'm wearing my protective jewelry, and my altar is protected. That's why I do those things ... because, being real with you, I get a little scatterbrained.

Note: Before I call the corners, I light my candles and incense, and ring my bell(s).

When I call the corners, I simply say:

"I call the elements, my spirits, my ancestors, and my gods and goddesses of the North, South, East, and West."

When I'm done with my spell or the spell work I'm doing, I say:

"I thank my spirits, ancestors, gods, and goddesses of the North, South, East, and West—I release you."

If you would like a more traditional phrase to repeat, chant, or call upon during your practice, I suggest the following two books:

- For my **Black practitioners**, I recommend *The Black Woman's Little Book of Spells* by V.C. Alexander.

- For my **other practitioners**, I suggest *The Modern Witchcraft Grimoire: Your Complete*

Guide to Creating Your Own Book of Shadows by Skye Alexander.

Both books offer great examples of traditional chants, invocations, and structure to help you feel more grounded in your magical workings.

7: Cleanses

Let's talk about cleanses, they're one of my most favorite things to create. They have so many uses and are honestly so fun to make. I love stirring and bubbling my caldron ... all right, fine ... it's a pot. You understand the visual I'm going for.

There are four main cleanses I make: Florida Water, Rose Water, Home Protection Brew, and Moon Water. I use these cleanses daily and often. You can put them in small or large spray bottles or even Mason jars. I make large batches, so they last me a while. It may cost a little more for supplies but you're making big batches so in the long run it's saving you money.

I'm sure you're wondering if you can just buy these already made. Of course you can. Just like you can buy ready-made food. I do not judge at all if you buy pre-made. Sometimes money and circumstance make it easier to buy something already made. Remember, my goal is accessibility for all.

Note: The spiritual and spell work portion of these cleanses will be featured at the end of this chapter.

FLORIDA WATER

I get this question often and it makes me laugh every time. "What the hell is Florida Water???" Ten out of ten times everyone thinks it's literally water that comes from Florida. Honestly, I don't blame them because the name is confusing. So, before we get into how we make it, here's a little history of what it is.

FLORIDA WATER: A BRIEF HISTORY AND SPIRITUAL USE

Florida Water. It's a timeless tool with countless uses in spiritual work. While recipes can vary, most follow a similar foundation a base of alcohol (usually vodka, though some prefer gin) blended with herbs, flowers, fruits, and sometimes essential oils.

Florida Water[1] is a cologne first created in 1808 by Robert I. Murray, named after the legendary Fountain of Youth, said to be located in Florida. It combines citrus oils like orange, lemon, and bergamot with spices such as clove and lavender, all suspended in an alcohol base.

Originally worn as a refreshing fragrance and aftershave, it quickly became a beloved household staple—and eventually, a powerful spiritual ally.[1]

Magical Uses: Florida Water has long held a place in Hoodoo, Santería, Espiritismo, Voodoo, and various folk magic traditions. It's cherished for its cleansing, protective, and uplifting properties. Here are some favorite ways to use it:

- Add to cleansing baths to wash away heavy, stagnant energy.
- Wipe down altars, tools, and sacred spaces for spiritual purification.
- Offer it to ancestors and spirits in a glass on your altar.
- Use as a protective spray for your home and personal aura.
- Incorporate into floor washes or diffusers to clear and bless your space.

1 Murray and Lanman. *Florida Water Cologne History.* Lanman and Kemp-Barclay & Co., Inc., Florida Water Lanman & Kemp

It's a simple, beautiful way to bless, protect, and attract positive energy.

My Working Recipe

There are many ways to make Florida Water. This is the one I'm working with right now.

WHAT YOU WILL NEED

1. Vodka
2. Cinnamon sticks
3. Clove (whole or "berries")
4. Dried roses
5. Dried jasmine
6. Dried orange peels
7. Dried lemon leaves (optional) – great for cleansing, clarity, and fresh starts
8. Lemon juice
9. Rosemary

INSTRUCTIONS

STEP 1: Fill a pot halfway with water and bring it to a boil.

STEP 2: Lower the heat to a simmer, then add 2 to 3 cups of vodka.

STEP 3: Toss in your chosen herbs, flowers, and fruit peels.

STEP 5: Let it simmer until the mixture smells fragrant and harmonious, with no sharp vodka scent.

STEP 6: Once cooled, I add a splash of Moon water for an extra touch of magic. (Sometimes I'll stir in a drop or two of essential oil—sandalwood is a favorite of mine.)

STEP 7: Strain and store in a mason jar, ready for your spells, sprays, or baths.

Note: This is just one version. The beauty of Florida Water lies in its versatility. Every practitioner's recipe is a little different. I'm already dreaming up my next batch.

Rose Water

You'll notice some overlap between this and my Florida Water recipe—many of my home brews share a similar base, especially the ones I make most often. There are many ways to make rose water, but here's the one I'm using right now

WHAT YOU WILL NEED

1. Vodka
2. A mix of dried and fresh herbs, flowers, and fruit peels:

o **Dried roses** (For love, healing, and emotional balance)

o **Dried Jasmine** (For dreams, love, and spiritual connection)

o **Dried Orange Peels** (For joy, luck, and uplifting energy)

3. Dried Lemon Leaves (optional) (For cleansing, clarity, and fresh starts)

INSTRUCTIONS

STEP 1: Fill a pot halfway with water and bring it to a boil.

STEP 2: Lower the heat to a simmer, then add 2 to 3 cups of vodka.

STEP 3: Add your chosen herbs, flowers, and fruit peels/leaves.

STEP 4: Let it simmer until it smells fragrant and the alcohol scent fades.

STEP 5: Once cooled, I add a splash of Moon water for an extra magical touch.

STEP 6: Strain and store in a mason jar.

STEP 7: Use in spells, sprays, or spiritual baths.

MOON WATER

Moon water is something I think you should always keep handy. Realistically, not everyone has the storage space to keep water for every cycle or astrology phase. Also, if your practice isn't heavily focused on the Moon, I wouldn't expect you to keep a giant collection.

I do think it's essential to have some Moon water handy for cleanses, brews, glamour magic, and certain spell work.

MOON WATER VS. FULL MOON WATER

Now, some witches who are very by the book will say full Moon water is more potent and powerful, and that's what you should use. I take a practical approach to Moon water. Simply setting out water at night allows it to absorb the Moon's energy, which is powerful enough to be beneficial for spell work and other uses. You don't need an extensive collection or to track every lunar phase; keeping some Moon water on hand is what matters most for cleanses, brews, glamour magic, and spell work. I will note that full Moon water, or water charged during certain astrology phases, is a little stronger but all Moon water carries power.

It's all based on your personal practice. If you're a cosmic witch* or an astrology witch,* then your Moon water practice may lean heavier and be more structured. If that's not your vibe, then flex it to fit how you work. For me, I do a lot of spell work at nighttime and by the Moon, so it's naturally strong for me in general.

My goal is that you use Moon water, not what kind of Moon water you choose.

***Note:** If you would like more information on types of witches and how to research it, I provide consultation appointments on my site. The consultation dives deeper into every subject mentioned in this book. I provide economic tiers for every income level.

WHAT I DO

I personally collect water for each astrology phase. I like to do this if I'm working on a spell where I need to connect to a certain element or sign. However, I'll also use any kind of Moon water. I'm not as particular as some witches are.

DRINKING MOON WATER

You can also drink Moon water. Some feel a spiritual and strong magical connection by ingesting the water. The water is often used in tea and cooking magic as well. If you do this, just make sure the water is safe and clean.

Home Protection Brew

——••••◇••••——

This brew follows a similar process to my Florida Water and Rose Water recipes. It's designed with protection, cleansing, and peace in mind.

WHAT YOU WILL NEED

This changes depending on what I have, but these are my go-to staples (I use a mix of dried and fresh):

1. Basil
2. Bay Laurel
3. Lavender
4. Roses (or petals)
5. *Lemon (medium or large)
6. Salt

*Note: Your lemon can be sliced, squeezed, or whole.

INSTRUCTIONS

STEP 1: Fill a pot halfway with water and bring it to a boil.

STEP 2: Lower to a simmer, then add your chosen herbs and flowers, plus the lemon and salt.

STEP 3: Let it simmer until it smells beautiful and well-blended.

STEP 4: Once cooled, I add a splash of Moon water to boost the energy.

STEP 5: Strain and store in a mason jar for use in spells, sprays, or around the home.

SPIRITUAL AND SPELL WORK

This ritual can be done alongside your rose water or home protection brew, turning a simple simmer pot into a full magical work.

STEP 1: Heat water on the stove.

WHILE THE WATER HEATS

STEP 2: Slice your lemon.

STEP 3: Carve your candle *(optional)*:
- Inscribe the word "Protection" into a white or black candle.
- You may also carve symbols that reflect your intention (e.g., a heart for love, a dollar sign for prosperity).

STEP 4: Prepare your altar or workspace:
- Place the candle in a holder on a heat-safe plate.
- Sprinkle herbs and flowers over and around the plate.
- Add any personal objects like charms or trinkets that hold meaning.
- Create a protective salt circle *(optional)*: Sprinkle salt around the plate or altar to contain the energy.

STEP 5: Once the water boils, reduce to a simmer or low heat.

CASTING THE SPELL

STEP 1: Clear your mind:
- Take a few deep breaths.
- Focus intently on your intention.
- Be specific and clear about what you are calling in.
- Allow the energy to flow through you, grounding and centering yourself.

STEP 2: Call the corners (if this is part of your practice). (Please refer back to chapter 6.)

STEP 3: Light incense (optional):
- Choose scents that match your intention (e.g., Bayberry for prosperity, Lavender for peace).

STEP 4: Ring a Bell (optional). (This helps clear and activate the space, as well as call in the spirits.)

STEP 5: Light the candle:

- As you light it, say aloud (or from the heart):
"May the universe and Mother Earth flow through me and back out. I ask for cleansing and home protection."
- Feel free to rewrite or personalize this phrase to better suit your spirit and situation.

STEP 6: Add ingredients to the pot

STEP 7: Stir clockwise and chant.

- As you stir, say:
"I call for cleansing and protection for this brew." (Repeat 3 to 5 times.)

STEP 8: Then, stir counterclockwise and chant:
"I remove the negative energy and negative blocks from this brew."

STEP 9: When finished, turn off the heat and allow the brew to cool completely.

8: Protection Spells

Protection spells are incredibly popular—and honestly, every witch and root worker is doing them in some form or another. There are so many different approaches to protection magic, and I've found that it helps to classify them into two main categories: **spells that *call in* protection and spells that create protective objects.**

Both types of protection work are powerful and in my experience, most practitioners use a combination of both.

This is an area where it's really easy to overspend. You'll think you need to buy all the things—jewelry, trinkets, mojo bags, sachets, altar décor—and over time, trust me, your collection will grow.

But you don't need everything all at once.

Keep it simple.

The first things I protected and made special were things I already had—items that were important to me, that I had collected over the years long before I even fully embraced witchcraft and rootwork.

Protection spells can get complicated—but you can always keep them very simple.

Spells That *Call In* Protection

These are spells where you're asking for protection over:

- Yourself
- Your surroundings or home
- A loved one
- Your pets (because our animal companions deserve spiritual care as well)

You can simply spray around your home and even outside, calling for protection, balance, and positive energy. It really can be as simple as that. Not everyone has the time or resources to perform a more detailed spell or ritual, and that's okay.

However, if you do have the time and interest, I've provided a more in-depth option below. It may seem like a lot of steps, but they're all very easy. It's mostly just a matter of setting aside some time. The ingredients themselves are affordable, and you can always add or remove elements based on your needs and what you have on hand.

WHAT YOU WILL NEED

1. Candle Stick (5 to 6 inches) (optional)
   - White: For all-purpose clarity and purity
   - or Black: For protection
2. Herbs and Flowers (choose at least 3, like:)
   - Basil
   - Bay Laurel
   - Lavender
   - Roses (or rose petals)
3. Lemon (medium or large)
4. Salt
5. Florida Water (optional): Adds extra cleansing power

6. Moon water or spring water (optional)
7. Incense (optional)
8. Pot (medium or large)
9. Bucket or bowl

INSTRUCTIONS

STEP 1: Boil the Water:
- o Fill a pot with regular water and bring it to a boil. (If using Moon water and Florida Water, leave space in the pot to add them later.)

WHILE THE WATER HEATS

STEP 2: Slice your lemon.

STEP 3: Carve your candle:
- o Inscribe the word *"Protection"* into your white or black candle (optional).
- o Optionally, carve symbols representing your intention (e.g., heart for love, dollar sign for prosperity).

STEP 4: Prepare the Altar:
- Place the candle in a holder on a heat-safe plate.
- Sprinkle herbs and flowers over and around the plate.
- Add personal objects like trinkets or charms if desired.

STEP 5: Create a Protective Salt Circle:
- Sprinkle salt around your altar or plate.

STEP 6: Reduce Heat: Once the pot reaches a boil, reduce to a simmer or low heat.

CASTING THE SPELL

STEP 1: Clear Your Mind:
- Focus intently on your intention.
- Be specific and direct about what you seek to manifest.
- Allow the energy of the universe to flow through you.

STEP 2: Call the corners (if part of your practice).

STEP 3: Light incense (optional).

STEP 4: Ring a bell (optional).

STEP 5: Light the candle.
  o As you light the candle, speak aloud: "May the universe and Mother Earth flow through me and back out. I ask for cleansing and home protection."
  (Feel free to personalize this phrase as desired.)

STEP 6: Add ingredients to the pot:
  o Add the lemon slices, herbs, and flowers to the pot. (Add Moon water and Florida Water if using.)

STEP 7: Stir clockwise and chant.
  o As you stir, repeat aloud 3 to 5 times: "I call for cleansing and protection for this brew."

STEP 8: Remove the herbs, flowers, and lemon. Turn off the heat and let the brew cool completely.

PROTECTION RITUAL

STEP 1: Create a protective mixture:
- o Mix leftover herbs, flowers, and salt together.

STEP 2: Sprinkle the mixture outdoors:
- o Scatter the mixture around your home's perimeter (e.g., doorstep, windows, property line).
- o As you sprinkle, say:

"I ask for cleansing and protection of my home."

STEP 3: Store the brew:
- o Once cooled, pour the brew into spray bottles or mason jars.

STEP 4: Use indoors and outdoors:

- o With spray bottles: Walk through your home, spraying and cleansing each space. Focus on areas like door frames, windows, and windowsills.
- o With a bucket: Use a cloth or sponge to wash down entryways and key areas.
- o Spray or pour the brew around your property's perimeter for extra protection.

STEP 5: Close the corners (if part of your practice).

You can absolutely be an everyday witch who does simple, powerful things.

Spells That *Create* Protective Objects

---•••◦⊗◦•••---

These involve crafting or casting spells *on* physical items to carry protection with you. This could include:

- Jewelry
- Trinkets
- Sachets or mojo bags
- Decor or altar items

I find that purchasing or making Florida Water is a great way to start when it comes to protection work. You can simply spray an object, your altar, or yourself while repeating a short spell or intention.

This is a great way to start or honestly, even stick with.

I repeat something as simple as *"I call for protection of this item."* I repeat it three to five times.

Note: I light my candle, ring my bell, and call my corners. I spray the space, and I also add the spray to a bowl or plate of salt.

Witchcraft doesn't have to be complicated or some huge, elaborate ritual.

You can absolutely be an everyday witch who does simple, powerful things.

9: Love Spells

Love spells are a true staple in witchcraft and are often featured in pop culture and media. There are so many love spells in witchcraft and Rootwork (Hoodoo).

Before I get into my thoughts on love spells, I want to take a moment to show respect to my ancestors, fellow witch practitioners, and root workers—past, present, and future.

A lot of traditional love spells involve having someone fall in love with you, keeping a lover, making sure your partner stays faithful, or causing the person you're interested in to lose interest in someone else. These themes have been common throughout time, and there are countless spells that cater to those desires.

When you're ready to find the love that truly nourishes you, that's the time to call it in.

These are not the kind of love spells I personally practice.

That's not to say those spells or the witches and root workers who cast them are wrong. Not at all. I have deep respect for the traditions and the practitioners who provide those services. But for me, those kinds of spells don't align with my values.

I'm a strong believer that you should never have to beg someone to be faithful, to stay in love with you, or to fall in love with you. You deserve better than that.

There are also many books on love spells if that's something you're drawn to.

So, what kind of love spells *do* I practice?

I'm all about empowerment.

My love spells focus on attracting love within yourself first and calling upon the spirits, ancestors, and gods (or God) to help bring the person meant for you into your life.

To be honest, I don't even recommend doing a love spell until you've done some work on yourself. Love spells aren't just about calling someone in, they're about making sure *you* are bringing your best self to them, just as you hope they'll bring their best self to you.

That doesn't mean you shouldn't date or explore love while growing. But when you're ready to find the love that truly nourishes you, that's the time to call it in.

WHAT YOU'LL FIND IN THIS BOOK

The two love spells I feature in this book focus on:

1. Finding self-love
2. Calling in the right love when you're ready

Both are simple, intentional, and cost-effective. You shouldn't need to buy a ton of supplies to do them.

Whether you're looking inward or outward, these love spells are designed to center *you* and your power—not desperation or control.

Self-Love Spell

WHAT YOU WILL NEED

1. Pink candle
2. Two pieces of paper (large enough to write a list on, but small enough to fold down)
3. Pencil (to write)
4. Plate or bowl
5. Heat-safe bowl or plate
6. Rose and jasmine flowers
7. Rose water (optional)
8. Incense (rose or jasmine)

INSTRUCTIONS

STEP 1: Dress your candle and write the word love on it.

(Review chapter 4 on candle dressing if needed.)

STEP 2: Prepare your altar. Sprinkle flowers on the altar and on the plate.

STEP 3: Call the corners and protective circle. Close corners after spell.
(Review chapter 6 if needed.)

STEP 4: Light the candle and call your spirits, ancestors, and god/gods/goddesses. Also light the incense.

STEP 5: On one piece of paper, write down all the negative aspects you want to work on and release—things you tell yourself.
Example: *I don't deserve love. I hate my body.*

STEP 6: Fold the paper three times toward yourself: fold down, rotate to the left, fold down, rotate to the left again, and fold down once more.

STEP 7: Place the paper in the heat-safe bowl or plate and light it on fire. Once the flame dies down, let the smoke blow out the window or door, releasing that energy from yourself and your space.

STEP 8: On the second piece of paper, write down all the positive self-love affirmations you want to invite in.

Example: *I am enough. I trust and believe in myself.*

STEP 9: Fold the paper three times toward yourself: fold down, rotate to the left, fold down, rotate to the left again, and fold down once more.

STEP 10: Place it on a bowl or plate and sprinkle more flowers on it.

STEP 11: Reflect on what's written on the paper daily. I suggest lighting the candle every day until you truly believe it.

SUGGESTIONS

Take a few minutes each day to practice meditative breathing and focus on the self-love you're trying to grow. If that's not your thing, I have other suggestions:

- Spray your mirror daily with rose water, wipe it down, and recite what's on the altar paper.
- During this time, ask yourself deep questions about why you're lacking self-love. Journaling can help, and if you're already in therapy or considering it, this is also a great time to get some outside professional perspective.

I'm a firm believer in spirituality and magic, but I also deeply respect medical professionals. Therapy and mental health support can work synergistically with your magic and spirituality. They can be a true gift for healing as well.

Love Spell

This love spell is designed for after you're already in a place of solid self-love. Whether you've performed the self-love spell listed above or you're just naturally there and ready to jump in.

Note: If you're now ready to do the love spell after completing the self-love spell, I want you to take that folded piece of paper you've had on your altar, place it in a heat-safe bowl, and light it on fire to release it into the world.

Similar to what we did with the negative aspects you were facing around self-love, once the flame is out, let the smoke flow out the window or the door.

WHAT YOU WILL NEED

1. Red candle
2. One piece of paper (large enough to write a list on, but small enough to fold down)

3. Pencil (to write)
4. Heat-safe bowl or plate
5. Rose and jasmine flowers
6. Rose water (optional)
7. Incense (Rose or Jasmine)

INSTRUCTIONS

STEP 1: Dress your candle and write the word love on it.

(Review chapter 4 on candle dressing if needed.)

STEP 2: Prepare your altar. Sprinkle flowers on the altar and on the plate.

STEP 3: Call the corners and protective circle. Close corners after spell.

(Review chapter 6 if needed.)

STEP 4: Light the candle and call your spirits, ancestors, and god/gods/goddesses. Also light the incense.

STEP 5: On a piece of paper, write down the following:

"I call for my future partner. A partner who is healed, a partner that is not only what I want but need."

STEP 6: Fold the paper three times toward yourself: fold down, rotate to the left, fold down, rotate to the left again, and fold down once more.

STEP 7: Place the paper in the heat-safe bowl or plate and light it on fire. Once the flame dies down, let the smoke blow out the window or door. Releasing that energy into the world and attracting your companion.

⎯⎯•••◈•••⎯⎯

In my personal opinion, I don't like the idea of obsessing over love. Constantly lighting a candle or focusing too hard on it. Much like the journey of self-love, it takes time.

What I do suggest is this: if you feel like you need to shake up that energy, light that red candle once a month. Or if absolutely needed, once a week. Sprinkle the flowers again and ask the spirits to continue bringing you the love you've called for.

But the key is to go on and continue to live your best life.

Note: You can also light a road-opening candle along with the love candle to amplify the energy and open the opportunity for love.

10: Money Spells

M uch like love spells, money spells are just as popular. There are *so many* different types of money spells—and so many different ways to perform them. It can get overwhelming and overcomplicated real fast.

If you take anything from this section, let it be this:

When it comes to a money spell, be clear about exactly what you're asking for. Make sure your reason is rooted in true intent, not just a surface emotion or deeper issue.

Most of the money spells I do now are based in Hoodoo. However, if my client is not of African American descent in some way, I will instead perform a non-closed-practice spell.

I'll be honest—I made the mistake early on of making money spells way too complicated. The spell I'll give you here is simple, concise, and hopefully includes herbs and spices you already have at home.

Another cost-cutting option? Buy a pre-made money candle or a basic green prayer candle.

Remember, it doesn't have to be complicated to be witchcraft.

A Simple Money Spell

WHAT YOU WILL NEED

1. One herb (like oregano or catnip)
2. Two spices (like allspice and nutmeg)
3. One candle (green or white)
(Check the Color-coded System for Spells in chapter 3 for all green/money related ingredients including optional flowers and fruit.)

BEFORE YOU BEGIN

In my practice—especially with spells for things like love and money—I believe in doing the emotional prep work beforehand.

I suggest sitting with yourself and asking:

What do I really need this money for?

You might be thinking, *Uh, Pam, I need money because I'm broke … duh.*

Valid! But let's go a little deeper.

If you're broke, okay. So with this extra money, what would it actually *do* for you?

- Are you looking for career advancement?
- Do you need a small cash flow boost to help you cover bills?
- Or are you asking for opportunities that will allow you to create more consistent income?

The clearer your request, the more success you're likely to have.

THE DAY BEFORE THE SPELL

I recommend lighting a road-opening candle.* If you don't have a road opener, use an orange candle (orange is great for opening energy and opportunities).

And of course, as mentioned in the candle section, if you don't have orange or green, white is always a solid backup. Just write "Road Opening" on the candle with a marker or carve it in.

While it burns, meditate on the idea of financial paths literally opening up for you. Sit with that feeling and think deeply about what you *truly* want.

***Note:** I use road-opening candles alongside other candles in spells almost every time—*except* when I'm doing protection spells or hexes. Protection work is about guarding your space and energy, not inviting things in.

I also wouldn't use road-opening candles for a hex. That's a whole different ballpark, in my opinion.

INSTRUCTIONS

STEP 1: Dress your candle and write the word *money* (or *abundance*, if preferred) on it.

(Review chapter 4 on candle dressing if needed.)

STEP 2: Prepare your altar. Sprinkle your chosen herbs and spices on the altar and on the plate.

STEP 3: Call the corners and protective circle. Make sure to close the corners after the spell.

Review chapter 6 on calling corners if needed.

STEP 4: Light the candle and call your spirits, ancestors, and god/gods/goddesses. You may also light incense if desired.

STEP 5: On the piece of paper, write down exactly what you need help with financially.

o   Some examples include:

"I call for $1,000 to help with a bill."

"I call for a promotion to help with money flow."

STEP 6: Fold the paper three times toward yourself: fold down, rotate to the left, fold down, rotate to the left again, and fold down once more.

STEP 7: Place it on a bowl or plate and sprinkle more of the spices and herb.

STEP 8: When your spell comes to fruition, make sure to either light that piece of paper on fire and release it, dispose of it off your property, or bury it in a garden—herbs and spices included.

EXTENDING YOUR SPELL

If you're asking for a *big* shift or financial breakthrough, be prepared: you may need to do a seven-day candle spell.

That means for seven days, you light a candle either:

- green tapers (7 total)
- white tapers (7 total)
- Or one green prayer/money candle that you light for several hours each day

Some practitioners let the candle burn all the way out each time or on the seventh day. Others save it and use it again. Do what feels right for *you*. Trust your intuition.

If you're working with limited resources and can't afford to use a full candle all in one go, that's fine! Let the candle burn for a few hours each day.

Note: Magic tapers are smaller and typically burn for 30 minutes to an hour so those can be safely used in full each day.

11: Hexes

Hexes, much like love spells, are well-known even to people who don't practice witchcraft. Because of how they're depicted in the media, they're often villainized, labeled as "dark magic" or "evil." This misunderstanding has deep roots in patriarchy and white supremacy.

Hexes are often misrepresented, even within the witchcraft community. There's the idea of the "Threefold Law" and loose interpretations of karma that lead some to fear or reject hexing altogether. But let's be real. Those who demonize hexes are often the ones already in positions of power. Of course, they'd vilify something that could threaten their control or challenge their abuse of power.

African Americans and African peoples have deep roots in hexing especially in Hoodoo. As a heavy practitioner of hexes, I believe they are about balance and energy. I don't believe in rigid binaries like "light vs. dark" or "good vs. bad" when it comes to magic. All energy is valid. All energy has purpose. And sometimes that energy isn't pretty.

Sometimes, a hex *needs* to be done.

Some of us, including myself, are more naturally drawn to hexing. That may be due to ancestral ties and our path as root workers. Other practitioners, like those who specialize in love spells or healing, may not be drawn to hexes—and that's completely okay. Hexing isn't for everyone. But I *do* believe it's essential for any practitioner to have a basic respect and understanding of what hexes are and what they're for.

Should we hex casually? Absolutely not.

Do I think we should be out here casting hexes *willy-nilly*? No. That's another common (and deliberate) misunderstanding.

Like any other spell, there's a time and a place.

I believe in:

- Hexing for the greater good.
- Hexing for those who've been truly wronged.
- Hexing when someone has done deep harm— to me or to those I care about.

Hexes and spells aren't just about personal gain. They're also about justice and protection. We, as practitioners, have a responsibility to care for the world around us. And sometimes, yes—you have to hex the patriarchy.

The hexes I personally perform are heavily based in Hoodoo and often require specialty items or more advanced ingredients.

The hex I *will* share here is more accessible and not rooted in Hoodoo. I've intentionally omitted or altered any elements that would make them specific to that tradition. This is a spell that anyone can practice, regardless of their cultural background.

I prefer performing hexes at night. That's when I feel most in tune with the energies around me. Some practitioners are early risers and work best at sunrise. You'll know when it feels right for you.

Before we go further, I want to note that crafting a hex isn't necessarily complicated, but the energy required can be quite intense. The bigger the hex, the more magic you might need—sometimes even help from another practitioner. That's why even experienced witches often seek assistance from someone more seasoned or ask for support. So if a hex doesn't work for you on the first try, that's okay—your magic just might not be there yet. However, if you're drawn to this section, you might have a natural affinity for hexing.

Hexes and spells aren't just about personal gain. They're also about justice and protection. We, as practitioners, have a responsibility to care for the world around us.

Freezing Jar Hex

WHAT YOU WILL NEED

1. Small container (freezer safe)
2. Small piece of paper (big enough to write a few lines, but small enough to fit in your container)
3. Pencil (honors the earth element and the energy around you)

4. Cayenne seasoning (or any hot seasoning, or hot sauce)
5. Black candle (preferred)
6. Moon water (optional)

BEFORE YOU BEGIN

Make sure your emotions are in check and that you're in a good place. It's okay to let anger fuel you, but make sure you're controlling the energy and magic—otherwise the spell may become chaotic in a way you don't want.

INSTRUCTIONS

Here's how I do it:

STEP 1: Light your candle, ring a bell, and call the corners.

STEP 2: Write the purpose of the hex on the piece of paper. (Be clear and decisive about what you need to stop or want to happen.)

STEP 3: Fold the paper three times towards yourself: fold down, rotate to the left, fold down, rotate to the left again, and fold down once more.

STEP 4: Place the folded paper in the container and sprinkle cayenne pepper, hot seasoning, or hot sauce generously on top.

STEP 5: Pour Moon water or regular water into the container until it's nearly full. Secure the lid tightly.

STEP 6: Shake the container five times until the water takes on the color of the spice you used.

STEP 7: Carefully swirl the container over the candle flame three to five times, saying the hex aloud each time. (You can let the hex sit for a few minutes to an hour, depending on how powerful you want it to be and what your intention is.)

STEP 8: Place the container deep in your freezer. (Some people put theirs in paper bags or hide them—just make sure you label it "Do Not Open.") The hex is now complete. Leave it in the freezer indefinitely, or until it has served its purpose.

STEP 9: When it's time to release the hex, defrost the container and pour the contents out in your garden, thanking the spirits for their help, or dispose of it in the trash respectfully.

12: Skin and Body Care

You may be asking: What do skin care and body care have to do with magic and spirituality?

Well, this is another form of witchcraft you can be drawn to. Even if it's not your main practice, it's something you can add to your routine when needed.

I often engage in simple forms of glamour magic, and I've highlighted some basic explanations below. Like other topics in this book, there are *plenty* of books dedicated to glamour magic. And yes, like anything else in the magical world, glamour magic can get expensive—but I'll say this over and over again: The magic is within you, and simple supplies can absolutely get the job done. You do *not* need to break the bank to practice glamour magic especially in its simplest forms.

——•••◈•••——

I'll say this over and over again: The magic is within you

——•••◈•••——

WHAT IS A GLAMOUR WITCH?

A glamour witch is someone who specializes in glamour magic and rituals. It's that simple.

What is a glamour spell or practice?

Kalyn Anderson of www.hauswitchstore.com describes it beautifully in her blog titled *Glamour Magic for Beginners*:

Traditionally, a "glamour" referred to a spell/ magical working that could change the spellcaster's appearance or the way others perceived them. Today, many modern practitioners use "glamour magic(k)" to refer to rituals of beauty that include magical intention.

Some include an element of shifting your physical appearance—but not all!

Glamour magic (at least the way I practice) is NOT about altering your appearance to better appeal to others OR conform to beauty/fashion norms.

In fact, it helps us escape these traps by allowing us to see our rituals of beauty and adornment as expressions and amplifications of our energy and intention.

In glamour magic, it's not important what shade or shape is most "flattering" or whether you wear white after Labor Day.

Does it feel like an expression of your personal magic and intention?

PERFECT. Go for it.

HOW I PRACTICE GLAMOUR MAGIC

I keep my glamour magic simple. It focuses on my inner and outer beauty and often blends in elements of protection and balance.

I use ingredients and herbs that align with my goal, paired with a short, spoken spell repeated three to six times. I perform this during regular skin care rituals—like washing my face, removing a face mask, or applying my serums and lotions.

When I'm in the shower, I'll use a homemade body scrub and say a spell as I apply and rinse it off.

ONE OF MY GO-TO GLAMOUR SPELLS

While working *clockwise* on my skin, I say:

"I call in positive energy. I call for balance. I call for my inner and outer beauty to shine."

(Repeat 3 times.)

Then, while working *counterclockwise*, I say:

"I call for the removal of negative energy and negative self-talk."

(Repeat 3 times.)

Do the words vary sometimes? Absolutely.

If I feel like I need extra protection or stress relief, I adjust the wording. It depends on my mood, what I need emotionally, and what my skin needs physically.

ABOUT MY SCRUBS

I use very simple ingredients in my homemade scrubs because I have sensitive skin. You can always customize with extras—like lemon or other citrus—but I personally keep it gentle.

Common ingredients I use in my scrubs include:

- **Lavender** (calming)
- **Aloe** (healing and soothing)
- **Chamomile** (gentle, relaxing)
- **Carrier oil** (like jojoba or almond)

Summer Body Scrub and Spell

Below, I've included one of my most used and simplest homemade scrubs for your own glamour practice.

SUN-SOOTHING SUMMER BODY SCRUB + SPELL

WHAT YOU WILL NEED

1. One medium mason jar or container
2. One mixing bowl
3. Unscented aloe gel (fresh aloe from a plant works beautifully, too)
4. Salt (exfoliates)
5. Sugar (exfoliates)

6. Honey (hydrates and softens)

7. Dried lavender (repels negative energy, invites peace and calm) (No lavender? Substitute with lavender essential oil)

8. Dried rosemary (protection and purification) (No rosemary? Substitute with rosemary essential oil)

9. Carrier oil* (suggested oils: almond, coconut, or shea)

(*This might be the only thing you need to purchase. A good-sized bottle will last you a while and usually runs $10–$20.)

INSTRUCTIONS

STEP 1: In a mixing bowl, combine 1 cup sugar and 1 cup salt.

STEP 2: Add half a cup aloe gel (feel free to use more if you'd like a more gel-like texture).

STEP 3: Gently crush your herbs/flowers using a mortar and pestle or the bottom of a glass or jar. Add the herbs/flowers to your bowl.

STEP 4: Add 1 tsp honey.

STEP 5: Pour in half a cup of your chosen carrier oil (adjust as needed).

STEP 6: Mix all ingredients until you achieve a well-combined, yet coarse texture.

STEP 7: Transfer your scrub to a jar or container. Label it with the date—it should stay fresh for about a month. I suggest storing in the fridge.

WITCHY RITUAL PORTION

STEP 1: Light your candle and incense before beginning. Set your intention and goal for this scrub—what energy do you want it to carry? Ring your bell (if it's part of your practice) to call on your spirits, deities, or ancestors.

   o   Suggested call:

"I call upon my spirits and ancestors. Assist me with the magic of this healing scrub."

STEP 2: As you mix, speak your intention aloud while stirring clockwise.
   Suggested spell: "I command for healing and soothing with this scrub."

STEP 3: Stir three times, saying "renewal," and then three times, saying "refresh."

STEP 4: You may allow your candle to burn out naturally or gently blow it out.

STEP 5: Don't forget to thank your spiritual helpers for their guidance.
   (When using your scrub, repeat your spell or intention to reinforce the energy.)

Important Notes:
• **Do not bring glass jars into the shower!** Scoop a small amount into a bowl or cup before showering.

- This is a body scrub only. Do not use it on your face.
- Avoid using on sensitive areas.
- Wash all bowls and tools thoroughly after making the scrub to avoid cross-contamination with food items.

Skincare Disclaimer

There's already an overall disclaimer at the start of the book, but I will add specifically here: The skincare information, tips, and products shared here are intended for general informational and self-care purposes only. They are not a substitute for professional medical advice, diagnosis, or treatment. Everyone's skin is different—what works for one person may not work for another.

Please perform a patch test before using any new product to check for allergic reactions or sensitivity. If you have a known skin condition or experience irritation, consult a licensed dermatologist or healthcare provider.

Use all products at your own discretion and risk.

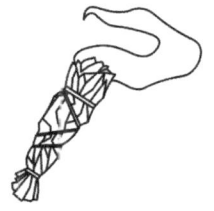

13: What's Not in This Book–and Why

WHERE'S THE SAGE?

As you may have noticed throughout this book, I've deliberately excluded the protection herb white sage. It's extremely popular in both witchcraft and Indigenous culture. Because of that, it's also in high demand and has become heavily commercialized.

Have I used it in the past? Yes.

Do I use it now? ... Also yes—but only because I purchased a large stock before I fully understood the deeper history behind it. Once my current collection is gone, I will no longer be using it in my practice whatsoever.

Indigenous peoples have asked us to stop using it. This is their sacred herb, and it's being depleted and commercialized to the point where even they struggle to access it.

As someone who comes from the closed practice of Hoodoo, I feel a deep responsibility to honor and respect other cultures—especially when they ask that we not use something sacred to their tradition.

There *are* alternatives that are more widely available for cleansing. For example, I personally love using chamomile bundles, as well as rosemary and lavender.

Some Indigenous communities say that if you must use sage, you should buy it directly from them. Others have asked us to stop using it entirely. I've chosen to honor the latter.

Note:

We've also been asked not to use Palo Santo and Sweet Grass. I don't use them at all.

For more on this overall topic, I highly encourage you to read books on Indigenous spirituality—written *by* Indigenous authors.

WHAT ABOUT CRYSTAL WITCHES?

Trust me—I have *high* respect for crystal witches and the energy surrounding crystals. My sister is actually a crystal witch and has a beautiful, growing collection. I love hearing her talk about the energy, how she's drawn to certain stones, and how that energy moves in and around her.

Like a tarot deck, crystal energy is a synergistic relationship between you and the stones—and I deeply respect that.

So why are crystals missing from this book?

This is a twofold answer.

First, crystals *can* be a wonderful thing to collect, but there are just *so* many out there that do all kinds of amazing things. I didn't want people rushing out to buy a bunch of crystals they may never use—or realizing later that crystals aren't actually magical tools that work for them.

Second, while some crystals are cheap, good quality, authentic crystals can get expensive. Unfortunately, the market is full of imitations and fakes, and it can be overwhelming or discouraging, especially for beginners.

Do I use crystals in my practice?

Yes, I do—but they aren't the main player. I personally use amethyst, rose quartz, selenite, black obsidian, moonstone, and garnet. I use them in personal work and in spells where I want to *amplify* an intention. I'll also include crystals in custom spells for clients *if* they specifically request them. But for the reasons mentioned above, I don't typically offer crystal work as a standard part of my practice.

As always—if you feel a strong calling toward crystals, trust it. Just make sure to get a *detailed and informative book* before diving in and starting your collection.

I made this mistake myself early in my spiritual journey. I bought many crystals and crystal chips thinking I was going to be all about that crystal life. But once I really sat with them, I realized I only felt *mildly* drawn to their energy.

After buying a bunch of supplies and *then* doing deeper reading, I realized crystals were going to be more of a supporting tool for me, not a central part of my magic. I could have saved myself a lot of money if I had just started with a good book instead.

I recommend the book *The Crystal Bible* by Judy Hall. My crystal witch sister has found this book extremely helpful and highly recommends it.

WHY NO ASTROLOGY GUIDE?

The answer is very simple: I'm not a bullshitter—astrology is beyond me.

Astrology is incredibly detailed. I have a *profound* respect for those whose magic, witchcraft, and spirituality are rooted in it. But I would be doing both you and myself a disservice by trying to speak deeply on the subject.

I've been learning about astrology for years and still feel like I've only scratched the surface. I have a decent understanding of my Big 6 and the zodiac signs in general—but it goes *so much deeper* than that.

Honestly, I feel like I could study it for another ten years and *still* keep learning new things.

Now, I do incorporate astrology into my magic—*lightly*. Mostly just by personalizing spells based on someone's sun sign or the elemental associations tied to that sign. But that's about as deep as I go right now when it comes to blending astrology and magic.

There's just *so* much to learn, and it's one of those topics where you could end up buying a ton of books—and that goes against what I'm trying to do with this book.

You might be thinking:

Great, Pam, that's fantastic. But how do I learn more about astrology without spending a bunch of money on books I won't understand?

A valid question. And I say that because I've *been there*. I bought a few books early on and just ended up confused, because I didn't even know where to start. It's all so detailed and layered.

What helped me most was getting my *birth chart* done—not just a basic one, but a detailed one that broke everything down in a way that actually made sense. It gave me a clearer idea of which areas of astrology I wanted to explore deeper, and it helped me better understand the books I *did* end up reading.

Here's my recommendation:

Look for a practitioner who offers detailed birth chart readings—either through a trusted spiritual shop or Etsy.

If you go through Etsy, make sure to read the reviews so you know how detailed and helpful the chart actually is. This is a great way to explore astrology *without breaking the bank*.

Yes, some people will say you *should* only go to someone in person who specializes in astrology at a spiritual shop. And I get it—practitioners deserve to be paid fairly for their work. But I also know that not everyone can afford to spend $50 to $130 (or more) on a chart reading.

So, if Etsy is what's accessible to you, that is *absolutely* valid. I've seen some amazing, detailed charts go for around $12 or even less.

Don't ever let anyone tell you you're less of a witch or spiritual practitioner because you took an economic shortcut.

Spirituality and witchcraft are for *everyone*— not just those who can afford fancy tools and high-end services.

Spirituality and witchcraft are for everyone.

WHAT IS A CLOSED PRACTICE?

The friendlystreetwitch.com explains it well.

It is a form or type of witchcraft or other magical art that is associated with a culture that has been oppressed. This could be the Native American practices, the Hoodoo and Voodoo cultures, the Oshun, even Gardnerian Wicca is technically a closed practice as you need to go through a lengthy initiation ceremony to practice it.

The reason we consider these closed practices is for one of two reasons, either because it is a religion that needs an initiation to practice (such as Wicca) or because the members of that culture have had so much taken from them, we let them choose who practices it out of respect (such as the Native American practices).

TEA AND COOKING MAGIC?

I love drinking and cooking magic and incorporating it into everyday use. It's something I'm so passionate about. But I felt like I couldn't give it proper justice by only doing a small section in this book.

I actually have future plans to create a book solely focused on this—similar in style to this one, with reference guides and ways to keep the cost low.

In the meantime, just remember you can incorporate magic sayings, like I did in the skincare glamour section. You can stir your tea, coffee, or whatever food you're mixing while asking for protection, calm, or whatever you need from it. Stir clockwise to draw in energy, and counterclockwise to remove any negative energy that may be in and around you.

That's a very simplistic, light dusting of what working magic through food and drink can be—but I wanted to give you something to start with.

14: Practical Matters

BUYING SPELLS VERSUS DIY

You might be wondering about the difference between buying a spell, versus paying someone to do the spell, versus doing it all yourself. What is better?

As you've noticed throughout this book, I keep it honest. I do not have an answer for you. The answer for that is within you. This is a topic that is often debated. I do have some thoughts, though. Sometimes a spell is a little bit bigger than we are trained for, and you may need the help of a more seasoned practitioner. Paying for them to do the spell is ideal. Some witches and practitioners aren't as great with spell creation—

that's not what they specialize in. So, they may seek the help of a witch who already has a spell made and then perform it themselves.

Lastly, some people just don't have the space to perform spells and cannot collect all the resources for it. For them, paying a practitioner to do the spell is also an option. I don't think that's bad either. Historically, that's very classic. And there's nothing wrong with switching between all those options. You will know what's best for you.

SHOPPING FOR WITCH SUPPLIES

When it comes to spiritual shopping on Etsy and Amazon for Witch supplies, here are my thoughts and a bit of advice.

Spiritual shops and Etsy are ideal—they support small businesses, and you can have a better understanding of where your products are sourced from. Etsy also has some reasonable pricing.

But I'm not here to be an elitist. There are circumstances where people don't have the time or the resources to curate individual items from Etsy or visit a spiritual shop. This could be due to a lack of resources, transportation, or physical limitations.

I do not, once again, work in absolutes—and I do not judge if you get your stuff off Amazon. Just remember you don't need to have the entire collection right away. We should be building it slowly, anyway.

This is what I *should* have done—but I didn't. I think it's my Aries nature.

Note: Keep in mind that Etsy isn't perfect—there are sellers on there who aren't small businesses. So, you really have to do your research, look carefully, and make sure to read the reviews.

CANDLE ISSUES

What happens if a candle will not light or glass breaks?

Sometimes, when a candle won't light or a glass breaks, it's a sign that now isn't the right time to perform the spell. Something may be working against you or blocking your path. Of course, always use your best judgment: if you're somewhere windy, it's natural for a candle to have trouble. And if you're not following safe candle practices, that might be why the glass breaks. But if none of those practical issues are present, it's definitely a sign to pause and reconsider doing the spell at this time.

OUTDOOR ALTAR SETUPS

For those wondering about outdoor altar setups: do you have to have one? No. Do I have one? Absolutely. I like to honor the spirits and gods that protect the outside of my home. When it comes to special Moon phases, I also like having an altar where I can place the Moon water I'm making.

Every outdoor altar is unique, of course. Personally, I like to collect rocks and arrange them around my altar, decorating them with special runes or symbols. On the table, I keep some outdoor incense burners. I also gather flowers, plants (especially herbs), and fruits or veggies from my garden to add to the space.

Then I bring out protective incense—like frankincense and myrrh—light them, say a little prayer, and thank the spirits and gods.

If you don't have that kind of space, that's completely fine. You can always sprinkle herbs, plants, or fruits just outside your door as a thank-you.

Note: Please do not leave incense unattended.

————•••◆•••————

There is no one way to do witchcraft.

————•••◆•••————

CLOSING NOTES AND THOUGHTS

There is no one way to do witchcraft—and that's the beauty of tapping into your spirituality. As you become more comfortable and go deeper into your practice, things will naturally change and grow. That's the beautiful part of the journey.

Remember: the magic is—what? Within you.

Lastly, if you're buying this book secondhand—wonderful! I've bought many books secondhand myself, and I'm happy to contribute to the life and legacy of beautiful used books across the U.S.

BOOK RECOMMENDATIONS
FOR A DEEPER DIVE

Herbal Magic: A Handbook of Natural Spells, Charms, and Potions by Aurora Kane

The Green Witch: Your Complete Guide to the Natural Magic of Herbs, Flowers, Essential Oils, and More by Arin Murphy-Hiscock

The Modern Witchcraft Grimoire: Your Complete Guide to Creating Your Own Book of Shadows by Skye Alexander

The Crystal Bible by Judy Hall.

For Black practitioners:

The Black Woman's Little Book of Spells by V.C. Alexander

Rootwork: Using the Folk Magick of Black America for Love, Money and Success by Tayannah Lee McQuillar

Hoodoo For Beginners: Working Magic Spells in Rootwork and Conjure with Roots, Herbs, Candles, and Oils (Hoodoo for Life) by Angelie Belard

ACKNOWLEDGEMENTS

A huge thank you to my mentor Lindsay Melnick (The Florida Witch) whose ethereal soul, fiery energy, and sharp wit helps guide me on my witchy path.

https://linktr.ee/floridawitch

A shout-out to the amazing Jaime McNeil who did an amazing and beautiful job on the cover and art in this book.

Instagram: @cosmic.pancake

A big witchy hug to the wonderful Katie Fruits for her kind words on this book.

https://www.etsy.com/ca/shop/LoreAndBramble

Big Hugs to Bethany Kelly for her amazing guidance through this book. Thanks also to my book editor, Anaik Alcasas and my book designer, Stefan Merour.

https://www.publishingpartner.com/

CONNECT WITH THE AUTHOR

You may have read through this entire book and still be thinking, *Pam, help!* That's exactly where I come in. (Shameless self promotion alert!) On my website, I don't just provide tarot readings; I also offer a variety of other services. These include both pre-made and custom spells. I can even cast and perform on your behalf.

One of my most popular services is consultations. These are flexible, tailored to your needs, and I'm mindful of economic accessibility. A consultation might involve diving deeper into the topics touched on in this book, guiding members of the Black community through Rootwork and/or Voodoo, or simply helping you find the direction you want to take within your spiritual or witchcraft practices.

In addition, my website features announcements and monthly blog posts. The blog is a space where I share deep dives into witchy topics, special spells, magic food recipes, and socio-political issues that matter deeply to me and my community.

I look forward to connecting further with you.

Visit my website and Instagram for more information.
Instagram: @Ladybugdivinationandspells